PIRATE QUEENS

NOTORIOUS WOMEN OF THE SEA

JOHN GREEN

DOVER PUBLICATIONS, INC.
MINEOLA, NEW YORK

Inside this exciting coloring book you will find the pictures and stories of twenty-seven amazing women, women who happened to be pirates! From Artemisia, an ancient Persian Queen, to Grace O'Malley of 16th Century Ireland, to Huang P'ei-me in modern China, you will discover how all these women became feared warriors and rulers of the sea. So get your crayons, colored pencils, and markers ready as you embark on a seafaring journey through maritime history!

Bibliographical Note

Pirate Queens: Notorious Women of the Sea is a new work, first published by Dover Publications, Inc., in 2014.

International Standard Book Number

ISBN-13: 978-0-486-78334-5
ISBN-10: 0-486-78334-0

Manufactured in the United States by LSC Communications
78334004   2018
www.doverpublications.com

PRINCESS SELA, 400 AD, Norwegian. Princess Sela was the sister to Koller, King of Norway. She took to the sea as a pirate after her much-despised brother took the throne. She led many raids and amassed quite a fortune in treasure.

ALFHILD, 850 AD, Swedish. Alfhild was a Swedish princess who took to sea to avoid an arranged marriage. She commanded a small fleet of ships manned by both men and women and preyed on vessels in the Baltic Sea and on Danish coastal villages.

LAGERTHA, 870 AD, Viking. According to the medieval historian Saxo, Lagertha was a Viking shieldmaiden and wife of the legendary warrior Ragnar Lothbrok. Piracy was a way of life for the Vikings, and women would often take part in raids.

AETHELFLAED, 900 AD, English. Aethelflaed was known as "The Lady of the Mercians." She was the eldest daughter of King Alfred the Great of England. She took command of the English fleet after her husband's death to rid the seas of Viking raiders.

JEANNE-LOUISE DE BELLEVILLE, 14th century, French. Jeanne-LouiseDe Belleville, known as "The Lioness of Brittany," was a French woman who became a pirate to avenge the execution of her husband. She attacked only French vessels.

ELISE ESKILSDOTTER, 15th century, Norwegian. Elsie Eskilsdotter was a politically active noblewoman who took up piracy with her two sons in 1460 after her husband was assassinated. They declared open warfare and no mercy against the merchants of the city of Bergen.

GRACE O'MALLEY, 16th century, Irish. Grace O'Malley was born in Connaught on the west coast of Ireland. She was the daughter of a clan chieftain. Upon his death she inherited his large fleet of ships and his trading business.

O'Malley exacted tolls from vessels around the Irish coast and supported the Irish rebellions against the English. In 1593 she met with Queen Elizabeth l.

SAYYIDA AL HURRA, 16ᵀᴴ century. Al Hurra was a Moroccan of Andalusian descent. She ran a fleet of ships in the Western Mediterranean where she wreaked havoc on the Portuguese shipping lines.

LADY MARY KILLIGREW, 16TH century, England. Lady Killigrew was a member of the English aristocracy and was married to Sir John Killigrew. They had the permission of the Royal Court to operate fleets of pirate ships up and down the coast of Britain.

JACQUOTTE DELAHAYE, 17TH century, Caribbean. Jacquotte Delahaye was the daughter of a Frenchman and a Haitian woman. She was considered a great beauty who became a pirate after her father's murder. Once Delahaye faked her own death to avoid capture and lived as a man for some years before returning to piracy. Because of that and her red hair, she became known as "Back from the Dead Red."

13

ANNE DIEU-LE-VEUT, 17TH century, French. Anne Dieu-le-Veut was one of only a few woman pirates who operated in the Caribbean during the Golden Age of Piracy. She attacked Spanish vessels and reputedly took whatever she wanted. Dieu-le-Veut was not her real name; it was a nickname which means "God wills it" in French.

14

CHRISTINA ANNA SKYTTE, 17TH century, Swedish. Christina Anna Skytte was a member of the Swedish nobility who followed her brother into piracy. They attacked and terrorized ships of all nations on the Baltic Sea.

CHARLOTTE DE BERRY, 17TH century, English. Charlotte de Berry was supposedly born in England in 1636 and grew up dreaming of a life at sea. She married a sailor and, disguised as man, joined him on board his ship. However, her husband was accused of mutiny and flogged to death. De Berry then killed the officer responsible and fled, eventually turning to piracy. Although her story is well known, many experts today consider it to be untrue.

INGELA GATHERHIELM, 18th century, Swedish. Ingela was married to Lars Gathenhielm, who had received permission from the King of Sweden to attack and plun-der ships from enemy nations on the Baltic Sea. Upon his death in 1718, she took over his privateering and pirate empire.

ANNE BONNY, 18TH century, Irish. Anne Cormac was born in County Cork, Ireland, and was raised in America in the Carolinas. She married James Bonny, a common sailor. They moved to Charles Town in the Bahamas where she met Jack "Calico Jack" Rackham. She eventually left her husband to join Rackham on his pirate ship.

MARY READ, 18TH century, English. Mary's mother disguised her as a boy when she was a child in order to receive support from her paternal grandmother. Mary continued this deception on-and-off her entire life. In 1720 she joined Jack Rackham and his companion, Anne Bonny. No one knew Read was a woman until Anne began to take a liking to her. Rackham became jealous so Mary revealed her true identity. Rackham then allowed her to remain as part of the crew.

MARY CRICKETT, 18th century, English. Mary Crickett attacked and plundered ships off the coast of New England and for a time sailed with Captain Kidd. She was eventually captured and transported to the colony of Virginia were she was convicted of piracy and hanged.

FLORA BURN, 18th century, English. Flora Burn first joined a pirate crew in 1741, and eventually became captain of her own ship. She and her crew plied their terror on the Eastern Seaboard of America, plundering British and American vessels.

RACHEL WALL, 18TH century, American. Rachel Schmidt was born in Pennsylvania, and is considered the first American-born woman to become a pirate. She and her husband George Wall and their crew worked in the Isle of Shoals, off the New Hampshire coast. Between 1781 and 1782 they captured twelve boats, stole $6,000 in cash, and killed twenty-four sailors. She was eventually arrested and hanged on October 8, 1789.

CHING SHIH, 19th century, Chinese. Ching Shih was married to the pirate Zheng Yi and took command of over 300 ships after his death. She plundered British, Portuguese and Chinese vessels. By 1808 Ching Shih had built up perhaps the most powerful pirate fleet in history, with an estimated two thousand ships and 70,000 sailors.

JOHANNA HARD, 19th century, Swedish. Johanna Hard was a widow living on Vrango, an island off the Swedish coast. She took up pirating with her farmhand Anders Andersson. They were put on trial in 1823 along with three associates and accused of having attacked, plundered, and killed the crew of a Danish ship, the *Frau Mette*. Two of her crew were executed, but Johanna was released due to insufficient evidence.

CHARLOTTE BADGER, 19th century, English/Australian. Although born in England, Charlotte Badger is considered to be Australia's first female pirate. She was sentenced to seven years penal servitude in New South Wales, Australia, for theft. In 1806, at the end of her sentence, she boarded a ship named *The Venus* as servant and soon persuaded the crew to mutiny against the captain.

SADIE FARRELL, 19th century, American. Sadie Farrell was a notorious gang leader in New York's "bloody" Fourth Ward. She was known as "Sadie the Goat" because she headbutted her victims before robbing them. Farrell led a small but vicious crew that attacked schooners and small boats and also pillaged small villages up and down the Hudson and Harlem rivers.

LO HON-CHO, 20th century, Chinese. Lo Hon-cho was young and pretty but very ruthless. She gained a reputation as being one of the most dangerous pirates in the South China Sea. She attacked coastal shipping, fishing fleets, and small villages. In 1922 a Chinese warship intercepted her pirate fleet and destroyed over forty vessels. Lo Hon-cho escaped the battle alive, but was later handed over to the authorities by the remaining pirates in exchange for clemency.

HUANG P'EI-ME, 20th century, Chinese. Huang P'ei-me was another very successful Chinese pirate. She at one time commanded over 50,000 pirates. She attacked and plundered ships all along the east coast of China and sold the people she captured into slavery.